GLAMOUR
TEES

GLAMOUR
TEES

15 fabulous designs from everyday t-shirts

LINDA ZEMBA BURHANCE

The Taunton Press

DEDICATION

TO JULIETTA, my grandmother, who gave me my first sewing machine.

The Taunton Press
Inspiration for hands-on living®

The Taunton Press, Inc.
63 South Main Street
PO Box 5506
Newtown, CT 06470-5506
e-mail: tp@taunton.com

TEXT: Linda Zemba Burhance
EDITOR: Tim Stobierski
COPY EDITOR: Candace B. Levy
ART DIRECTOR: Rosalind Loeb Wanke
COVER AND INTERIOR DESIGN: Sandra Salamony
LAYOUT: Sandra Salamony
PHOTOGRAPHERS: Alexandra Grablewski (beauty) and
                Scott Phillips (process)

The following names/manufacturers appearing in *Glamour Tees* are trademarks: Blue Moon Beads®, Champion®, Dritz®, Etsy™, Hobby Lobby®, Jerzees®, Jo-Ann Fabrics®, Michaels®, Offray®, PeelnStick™, Simplicity®, Walmart®

Library of Congress Cataloging-in-Publication Data

Burhance, Linda Zemba, author.
  Glamour tees : 15 fabulous designs from everyday T-shirts / Linda Zemba Burhance.
      pages cm
  Includes bibliographical references.
ISBN 978-1-63186-484-1
1. T-shirts--Juvenile literature. 2. Clothing and dress--Remaking--Juvenile literature. 3. Sewing--Juvenile literature. I. Title.
  TT675.B87 2016
  687--dc23
                                    2015032196

Printed in the United States of America
10 9 8 7 6 5 4 3 2 1

ACKNOWLEDGMENTS

I WOULD LIKE TO THANK the team of talented people at The Taunton Press who worked so diligently on this book. First, to Shawna Mullen, for seeing the original concept as current, contemporary, and viable. Second, to Carolyn Mandarano, for making it into a "big idea."

Thanks to Rosalind Loeb Wanke for art direction and Sandra Salamony for design and layout. And of course, no design book would be complete without photography, so thanks to Scott Phillips for his great attitude and skill while shooting the process images and to Alexandra Grablewski for her stunning work and beautiful eye while shooting the beauty shots.

Last but not least, a very special thank you to Tim Stobierski, who edited the book, Candace Levy for catching all of my grammar and punctuation errors, and the *Threads* staff for the enthusiasm and support.

CONTENTS

INTRODUCTION

WE'VE ALL BEEN THERE: standing in the fancy boutique, looking at the designer T-shirt, feeling excited about trying it on, planning on where to wear it. And then we see the price—ouch! But you don't need to spend big bucks to get that designer look. You can have the same style at a fraction of the cost, and all it takes is a basic T-shirt and some store-bought trims.

This book offers inspiration and instruction for projects to create various types of glamour tees, ranging from simple to more elaborate. They all have one thing in common: They are spectacular looks that you can make yourself.

I have chosen to use standard T-shirts found in most national craft stores for the projects in this book. Most are 100 percent cotton and are very reasonably priced. I used a size medium or large junior fit throughout most of the book. I like the curvy female shape these T-shirts have. If you are more comfortable in a looser fit or in a long sleeve or a tank top, then buy that style of shirt as a base and use the instructions as a jumping off point. And, of course, you can use any brand T-shirt you prefer.

As for trims, I have chosen items that are also readily available in large national chains. However, if you have a favorite spot you like to shop or are a collector of vintage trims, go ahead and use whatever you like. Just make sure your trim items are washable by testing little snips in your washing machine before you begin a project.

If you feel like mixing or combining some of the different ideas in this book to create your own interpretations, go for it! Try a colored or patterned T-shirt as a base instead of a plain white or black one. Repurpose a favorite old T-shirt into something that you'll cherish for years to come. Use a different trim or a fabric with bling and make a statement with your look. It's your style. Have fun and make it your own.

Linda
xx

TOOLS

THERE ARE A few tools I think are great investments for anyone who sews, from a beginner sewing student to someone with vast sewing experience. These tools save time and will give you the professional results that you desire.

A **SELF-REPAIRING CUTTING MAT**

Cutting mats are an extremely valuable tool. I prefer to own two: a larger one (24 in. by 36 in.) and a smaller one (12 in. by 18 in.). The large one serves two main purposes. First, it provides plenty of room for you to lay out your T-shirts and do long, straight cuts, and second, it protects your tables, countertops, and other surfaces, especially if you don't have a dedicated workspace for sewing. The small one can be used for those quick cuts that most projects involve. Especially important for the projects in this book is the ability to place the smaller cutting mat between the two layers of your T-shirt: You will occasionally be making a cut to only the front or back of your garment, and the cutting mat will ensure that you do not cut through both layers.

B **ROTARY CUTTER**

There are no words to describe how easy it is to make a straight, clean cut, especially on a knit fabric like a T-shirt, with a rotary cutter. If you purchase only a couple of the suggested tools, it should be this one along with a cutting mat. Knits tend to "wiggle" when you cut them, and rotary cutters tame the wiggle. A rotary cutter is found in any craft or fabric store. I highly recommend trying this tool; you will see how simple and effective it is. It is so much easier to place the rotary cutter against a ruler or a French curve (see the next paragraph) and cut a sharp line or smooth curve.

 C **FRENCH CURVE**

A French curve is an essential tool that helps you make smooth and accurate curves while cutting. There are many projects in this book that require a French curve in order to cut out a neckline or curved hem. To use a French curve, just place the curve in position as directed and cut along the edge with a rotary cutter. You may need to adjust the position of the French curve to suit the size of your curve or the slope of your cut. Plastic French curves are very easy to use because they are see-through, which can help with things like centering a neckline curve or aligning a raw edge. A flexible ruler can also work and can sometimes be easier to find in stores.

D **VARIETY OF STRAIGHTEDGE RULERS**

A straightedge ruler and a right-angle ruler can really save time while you sew. Most cutting mats will have gridlines on them, which you can use to align your ruler to take the guesswork out of cutting a straight line. You can get by with a single, long straightedge ruler, but sometimes shorter ones can be easier to work with. You can also use multiple rulers in conjunction with each other to determine the position of a pin or trim to ensure accurate placement. You may also want a measuring tape, which is useful when measuring something while on the body.

E SCISSORS

Although I recommend using a rotary cutter for a knit fabric, I prefer to use two particular kinds of scissors in my sewing projects when it's necessary to use scissors. The first kind is called dressmaker's shears, which are very sharp and precise when cutting and are perfect for large, sweeping cuts. The second is commonly referred to as "snips," and they are specifically designed so that you can keep them in your hand while sewing because of their size and shape. You may also want to use small pointed-tip scissors for getting out that last small area of a deep V cut; and a seam ripper is handy to own as well, in case you make a mistake and have to rip out a seam. (Believe me, it happens to even the most experienced sewer.)

F PINS

I like to use dressmaker's pins since they have large, colorful heads and are longer in length than standard straight pins. The length of these pins helps when the fabric is one that tends to slide around because you can insert the pin into the fabric two or three times to really hold it in place. Although these are my favorite type of pins to use, any type of pin made for use in sewing will work.

SEWING MACHINE

I use a high-end computerized sewing machine with lots of fancy features, but for this book, all you need is a fairly basic machine that can do the following: a three-step zigzag stitch, a stretch stitch, and an overcast stitch. These are the basic stitches required for all of the projects in this book.

I find that the three-step zigzag stitch works great on knits because the stitch has a gentle give and works well with the inherent stretch of the knit. On my machine, I can also use a stretch stitch, which is a particular type of straight stitch with a little "mini zigzag" in it that is engineered specifically to use with knit fabrics. A stretch stitch is not available on every machine, but the three-step zigzag can be used just as effectively instead. I also use an overcast stitch for knits (this kind of stitch helps keep your cut ends from unraveling). If you are an expert sewer and have a serger, some of the seams in this book can be serged.

I also recommend a sewing machine needle that is designed specifically for use on knits. If your machine can be adjusted automatically for sewing knits, you should use that setting. You can check your sewing machine's manual to decide what works best for sewing stretch fabrics. Similarly, you should use thread that is compatible with your sewing machine, fabrics, and trims, so check your manual before beginning any project.

I hope you enjoy making these Glamour Tees as much as you enjoy wearing them. One thing is for sure—you will certainly have a glamorous T-shirt wardrobe when you are finished!

NOTES BEFORE GETTING STARTED

THE FOLLOWING ARE SOME THINGS to keep in mind before you get started on your projects; they will ensure an easier process and a more professional finish.

One of the ways to ensure your project is a great success is to prewash all of your items. You don't want to spend an afternoon creating a masterpiece, just to have it shrink in the first load of laundry. Wash and dry all of your garments before you do any sewing and then try on the shirt to make sure that it still fits the way you want it to. Even shirts that are labeled *prewashed* or *preshrunk* may shrink a bit during the first wash, so it is better to be safe than sorry.

I also strongly encourage you to read the washing instructions on all of the trims you are buying. The trims I used for the projects in this book are almost all machine washable, perhaps with one or two exceptions, but there are many trims available that either cannot be washed or need to be washed by hand. You should know this before you put the time and effort into creating your shirt.

I would also suggest that you familiarize yourself with the manual that comes with your sewing machine. There will be a section on how to sew knits as well as on thread suggestions. These are important bits of information that will help you sew items in a manner that will give you the best possible outcome. Certain types of threads work better in my machine than others, for example, and the manual spells this out. Taking the time to find out how your machine works the best is the secret to success. You can also ask for advice at your favorite craft or fabric store about which trim items may need a special thread.

I have used a few terms throughout this book that are industry-standard terms in the fashion business. For example, *right side wearing* **(RSW)** and *left side wearing* **(LSW)** are terms that refer to the garment as it appears on the body while you are wearing it. *High point of shoulder* **(HPS)** is the spot on the shoulder seam that is at the highest point (the point closest to the neck). Your shoulders angle down slightly from your neck to the top of your arm, and most of the time your shoulder seam will follow that line. The high point of the shoulders is the topmost part of that seam **(see Figure A)**.

Throughout this book, many projects will require you to **tack**. This simply means to hand- or machine-sew a stitch that will help stabilize the garment.

Last but not least, be sure to read the materials list and instructions before beginning any of these projects. There is nothing worse than getting halfway through a project and having to stop and run to the store to pick up a package of elastic or some self-adhesive tape. Make sure you have all of the materials before you begin to ensure a smoother process.

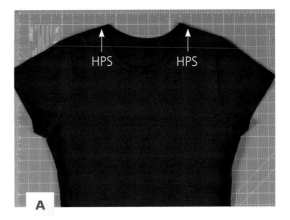

A

THE PROJECTS

PETTICOAT JUNCTION

Liven up your T-shirt wardrobe with this interpretation of the popular steampunk trend, which combines Victorian-era elements with modern-day avant-garde fashion. The results are wearable femininity with just enough "rebel" to balance out the look.

EXPERIENCE LEVEL

Intermediate

MATERIALS

Black 100 percent cotton T-shirt, such as Jerzees® ladies junior fit style (shown in size large)

1 or 2 (⅞-in. by 1-yard) packages of black ruffled elastic, such as Dritz® sheer ruffle elastic (amount depends on the measurement of the neckline)

4 yards of flowered netting trim (or enough to go around the T-shirt three times with slight overlaps at the cut ends, plus 12 in. for the shoulder details), such as 2-in.-wide 100 percent polyester Simplicity® Apparel and Craft

1 (⅝-in. by 20-foot) package of washable double-sided permanent fabric adhesive tape, such as PeelnStick™ Fabric Fuse

Matching thread for T-shirt and trims

TOOLS

Cutting mat

Pins

French curve or flexible ruler

Rotary cutter

Scissors

Sewing machine

Hand-sewing needle

1. Place the shirt face up on the cutting mat. Flatten out any wrinkles, perfectly matching the T-shirt front and back, so that when you cut the neckline, it is symmetrical. Align the bottom edges of the T-shirt together and with one of the gridlines on the mat; use a few pins to keep the T-shirt in place. If you have some paperweights, those are fairly effective as well. Just make sure that both of the HPSs are at the same line on the mat.

2. Place a pin at the center front of the manufactured ribbed neckline. Then place a flexible ruler or French curve in a pleasing and gentle slope, starting at the pin and working up toward the shoulder seam, just far enough away from the sleeve seam so that you do not cut the sleeve. This curve will determine the first half of the new neckline. Using a rotary cutter, carefully make a cut along the French curve, through both layers of the T-shirt **(Figure A)**. After you cut the first half of the neckline, flip the

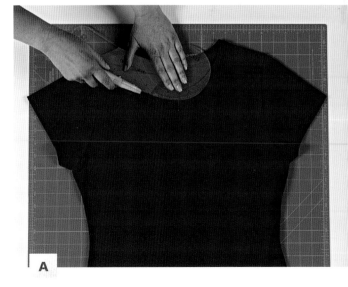

A

cut piece of T-shirt material to the uncut side so that you create a mirror image **(Figure B)**. The raw edge will also help you to align your French curve accurately **(Figure C)**. Cut the remaining side of the neckline.

I did not give measurements for how much material to cut off of the T-shirt for your neckline because you will want to size it to your tee and your body type. A rule of thumb is that you want to keep the raw edge of the neckline about ¾ in. away from the sleeve seam to make it easier to attach the ruffled elastic, but you can do a little more or a little less based on your preferences.

3. Use a three-step zigzag stitch on your sewing machine and matching thread to attach the ruffled elastic along the edge of the neckline. Take care to overlap the ends of the elastic because you want your neckline to look neat.

4. Measure off and cut three lengths of the flowered netting trim to go around the lower portion of your T-shirt as pictured; reserve the remainder for straps. Make sure to leave 1 in. or 2 in. extra for each cut length for overlapping the ends.

5. Following the manufacturer's instructions, apply the double-sided fabric adhesive tape to one length of the flowered netting trim. Attach by aligning the edge of the netting along the bottom edge of the T-shirt **(Figure D)**. Do this twice more, leaving about ⅛ in. between the rows of flowers. Sew the netting to the tee (see the Tips for more information).

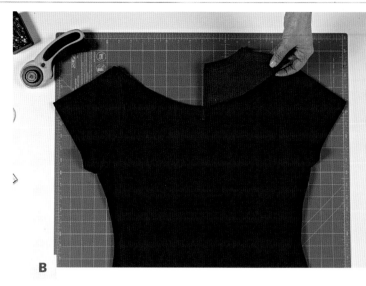

B

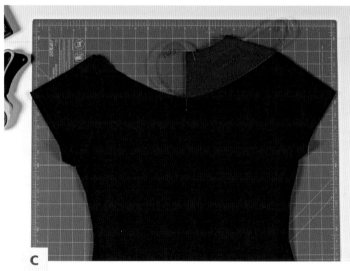

C

tip

I used the fabric adhesive tape as a substitution for basting thread because it is faster and more accurate to position the trim. However, you will still need to sew the trim onto the garment for permanency. Do not sew through the tape, which will leave adhesive on your needle and thread.

D

6. Try on the T-shirt and determine the position of the flowered netting trim for the shoulder straps. Mark the spot on each shoulder with a pin to indicate where you will place your straps. Cut two lengths of the flowered netting trim to create the straps (mine were approx. 6 in. long, but yours may be longer or shorter). Pin the flowered netting trim to the inside of the neckline where you marked the strap location, allowing 1 in. or so to hang down inside the shirt **(Figure E)**.

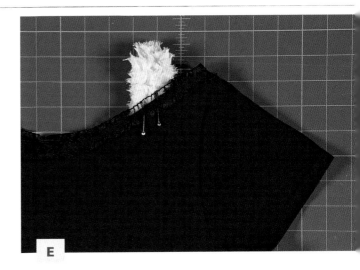

7. Topstitch the flowered netting trim to the neckline on the front and back of the shirt using a three-step zigzag stitch, making sure to match thread for a professional look. I used black thread on top and white in the bobbin thread. I was not worried about crushing the flowers here because the trim will be hidden inside the neckline. Snip any hanging threads—it's time to strut your stuff!

tip

Depending on what type of trim you choose, you will hand-stitch or machine sew. The flowered netting trim shown is very dimensional, and I didn't want to sew through and flatten the flowers by using the sewing machine, so I hand-tacked the trim inconspicuously in between the flowers. Although the style of the trim determines whether you sew by hand or machine, remember to sew on all trim to make sure it stays put.

variation

This project is shown in a black-and-white combination, but don't limit yourself to these colors. Try a soft pink with coral poppies or neon green with purple pansies. If flowers aren't for you, look for a trim with a geometric pattern for a modern twist or try sequins for a more glamorous look.

CUTE AS A BUTTON

The toss-and-sew process involved in making this T-shirt is inspired by a popular gardening technique called naturalization, where a gardener tosses flower bulbs onto the ground and then plants them where they land for a more natural-looking garden. This project is so quick and easy, you'll be outside enjoying the flowers in no time.

EXPERIENCE LEVEL

Beginner

MATERIALS

White 60 percent cotton, 40 percent polyester T-shirt, such as Champion® loose-fit Active Performance (shown in size medium)

1 or 2 (⅝-in. by 1-yard) packages of contrasting color shiny foldover elastic, such as Dritz black shiny foldover elastic no. 9389B (amount depends on the measurement of the neckline)

9 (2-piece) packages of premade ribbon and button flowers, such as Offray® no. 17989 100 percent polyester (number of packages depends on the size of the T-shirt and personal preference)

Matching thread for T-shirt and trims

TOOLS

Large and small cutting mat

Pins

French curve or flexible ruler

Rotary cutter

Scissors

Sewing machine

Hand-sewing needle

1. Place the smaller cutting mat inside the T-shirt and then place the T-shirt on the large cutting mat. You will be cutting out the front neck first, then the back neck. Place a pin at the center front of the manufactured ribbed neckline. Then place a flexible ruler or French curve in a pleasing and gentle slope, starting at the pin and working up toward the shoulder to make one side of the neckline. Cut along the French curve carefully using a rotary cutter, and cut through the manufacturer's ribbed neckline at the HPS to separate it from the tee.

Flip the cut piece of the T-shirt to the right side to use as a guide to create a symmetrical neckline curve and repeat the steps to create a mirror-image cut.

Do this by aligning the French curve to the raw edge of the flipped piece and cutting with a rotary cutter. You now have a pleasing and symmetrical front neckline.

To cut the back neckline, turn the T-shirt and cutting board over so the back side is facing up. Cut along the manufacturer's ribbed neckline using the rotary cutter and French curve, being careful to align the HPSs of both the front and back necks. After cutting the first half of the back neckline, flip the cut piece over to use a guide, as you did for the front.

2. Starting in the center of the back neckline, pin the foldover elastic to the neckline so the raw edge of the neckline is centered in the middle of the foldover elastic, as shown **(Figure A)**. This will give you room to fold the elastic down and encase the raw edge of the neckline later. Use a three-step zigzag stitch on your sewing machine and matching thread to attach the lower edge of the elastic to the neckline edge of the tee.

3. Then flip the foldover elastic down and topstitch it to the neckline, again using a three-step zigzag stitch **(Figure B)**. Be sure to overlap the elastic's ends in the back neck, so it will be inconspicuous. Trim the threads.

4. Remove all the premade flowers from their packages. Lay the shirt out flat, with the front facing up. Toss the flowers onto the front and pin them where they land. Of course, you can reposition the flowers to please your eye or place them however you like. Sew on the flowers using a hand-sewing needle and matching thread. I used a few tack stitches, but use whatever stitch will work for the flower buttons you purchased. You want the flowers to stay secure but the stitches to be inconspicuous.

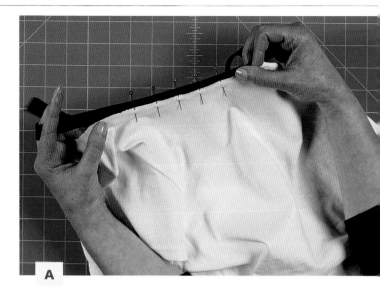

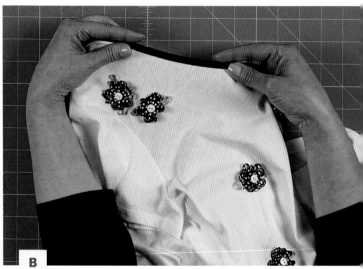

variation

If you prefer to leave the neckline of the T-shirt as is, go right ahead. If you prefer to use bigger flowers or large bright buttons instead of flower buttons, do that too. In any case, this tee will be cute as a button!

FLOWER ARRANGEMENT

*Crochet and lace are some of the hottest fashion trends around.
Interpret the trend into something unique by applying some
premade crochet flowers and cut lace to your plain old T-shirt.*

EXPERIENCE LEVEL	MATERIALS	TOOLS
Beginner	Black 100 percent cotton T-shirt, such as Jerzees ladies junior fit style (shown in size large)	Hand-sewing needle
	Seven 100 percent cotton premade crochet flowers in various sizes or handmade crochet flowers	Cutting mat
		Rotary cutter
	¼ yard of 55-in.-wide white all-over lace, such as Floral Scroll Lace (33 percent cotton, 24 percent nylon, 43 percent rayon), recycled lace, or lace scraps	Pins
		Scissors
	Matching thread for trims	Sewing machine

1. If you crochet, you can make the flowers yourself. If not, you can buy them premade from most craft and fabric stores or online. Select your flowers and group them together on the front of the T-shirt as you would like them to appear. I positioned mine to have a focal point traveling from one side of the neckline to the shoulder, but you can position yours however you like. When you are pleased with the positioning, hand-stitch them in place.

2. Cut out leaf shapes from lace. You can cut them freehand with a rotary cutter or use real leaves and a photocopier to create a template.

3. Pin the leaf shapes around the flowers in a way that looks natural and appealing and stitch them in place by hand or with a sewing machine and an overcast stitch. Use matching thread to the lace. Position some additional leaves along the bottom edge of your shirt (I chose to have my leaves on the hip opposite the neckline flower arrangement) and stitch them in place.

tip

If you want to attach the lace with glue instead of sewing it, make sure to choose a glue specifically for use on fabrics and be careful to use the glue where it will not show through the lace once it is dry.

variation

There are so many ways you can make this project your own. Imagine covering the whole upper half of the T-shirt with flowers and leaves or try keeping the torso blank and just covering the sleeves. Try a few designs before you stitch everything in place.

DESIGNER'S TWIST

Combine two tees and a curved edge adorned with some crochet or vintage lace to create an upscale version of a basic look. This T-shirt looks fantastic over skinny jeans or a pair of simple leggings. However you wear it, there is nothing plain about this white tee—it has a designer's twist for sure.

EXPERIENCE LEVEL

Intermediate

MATERIALS

2 white 100 percent cotton T-shirts, such as Jerzees ladies junior fit style (shown in size extra-large)

6 yards of ⅞-in. crochet lace edging, such as 100 percent cotton Simplicity Apparel and Craft (amount depends on the measurement of all the cut edges)

1 premade appliqué, such as Bliss style no. 29 felt and pearl daisy flower

Matching thread for T-shirt and trims

TOOLS

Pins

Cutting mat

Rotary cutter

Right-angle ruler and straightedge ruler or yardstick

French curve or flexible ruler

Scissors

Sewing machine

Hand-sewing needle

1. Mark the back of both T-shirts by placing a pin on one sleeve of each. You will not be cutting the sleeves, but you will need to remember which side of the shirt is the back.

2. Position one white T-shirt face up on the cutting mat. Place the other white T-shirt on top, face down, so the front sides are together. The back side of one shirt should be touching the mat and the back side of the other shirt should be facing you.

tip

Taking extra care to make sure both T-shirts are exactly aligned will create the most symmetrical mirror image in the final design.

3. Flatten out any wrinkles, perfectly matching the T-shirts' fronts and backs so that when you cut the hems, they are symmetrical. Align the bottom edges of the T-shirts together and with one of the gridlines on the mat; use a few pins to keep the T-shirts in place. Just make sure that all of the HPSs are at the same line on the mat.

4. Using a rotary cutter and a straightedge ruler, cut off the manufacturer's hemline. You want a crisp, straight raw edge to work with. Make sure to cut through all four layers (both T-shirts).

Using the manufacturer's ribbed neckline as a guide, position the French curve along one side of the front neckline. Cut through all four layers of the T-shirts at the neck very carefully using a rotary cutter, moving the French curve as you go to follow the stitching line of the collar **(Figure A)**.

5. Find the HPS and place a pin roughly 2 in. in from the shoulder seam on the right side of the flat garments. Align the long side of a right-angle ruler with the pin and make sure the short side of the ruler is parallel to the hem. **Note:** You can use an additional ruler to make sure the bottom of the right-angle ruler is indeed parallel to the hem. Make a straight cut from the pin to the hem, moving the ruler if needed but remembering to stay straight **(Figure B)**.

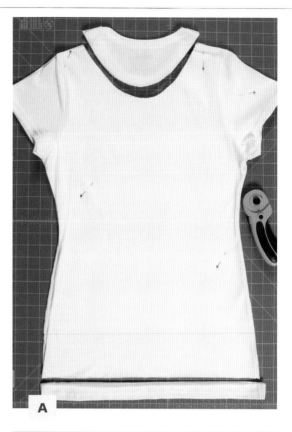

A

variation

Try using two different laces on each half of the shirt and a third one on the neckline for a bohemian flair. This is a great look to flaunt at your next outdoor music festival. Just make sure the lace is loose enough to be sewn on a curve; crochet laces are a great choice, and they definitely have that boho-chic vibe!

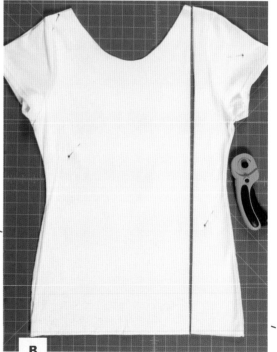

B

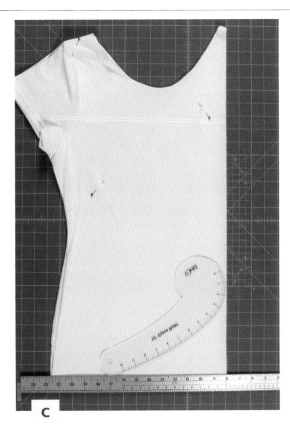

C

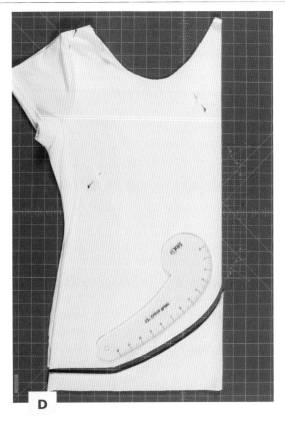

D

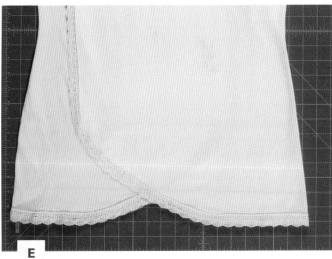

E

6. Place a flexible ruler on top of the bottom edge of the shirt, covering 1½ in. Find a point along the right angle raw edge. Position a French curve or flexible ruler at this point in a pleasing sweep, as shown **(Figure C)**. Cut along the French curve using a rotary cutter, making sure to cut through all layers of the two T-shirts, and then continue across the top edge of the flexible ruler **(Figure D)**. You should now have two cut shirt parts that have mirror-image curving hemlines.

7. Pin and sew the crochet lace along the curved raw edges of the two separate T-shirt halves using a sewing machine and an overcast stitch. Overlap the edges of the crochet lace and turn under any raw ends. You want your edging to look neatly finished. Trim any threads.

8. Place one T-shirt inside of the other so the curved lace edges are mirror images of each other, as shown **(Figure E)**. Place the overlapped shirt pieces on the cutting mat and flatten out any wrinkles so that the tees are perfectly aligned on front and back and all edges and pieces are lined up exactly.

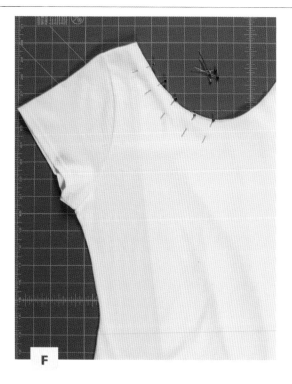

F

9. To keep the top in place when you are wearing the shirt, you are going to sew the crochet lace onto the neckline, capturing both of the T-shirts at once. To do so, pin the two tees together at the neckline and overcast the edge using the sewing machine **(Figure F)**. Then pin the necklines together to pre- pare for sewing on the crochet lace. Next, pin the crochet lace onto the overcast neckline and sew it in place using an overcast stitch. Tack a decorative flower on one shoulder by hand or machine. Trim any threads.

WRAP IT UP

What's black and white and cute all over? This project! Combine two shirts to create a high-fashion wrapped tee at a fraction of the designer brand cost. You can also try mixing things up with colored tees that complement each other or use lace instead of ribbon for a more feminine look.

MATERIALS

Black 100 percent cotton T-shirt, such as Jerzees ladies junior fit style (shown in size large)

White 100 percent cotton T-shirt such as Jerzees ladies junior fit style (shown in size large)

3 or 4 (⅝-in. by 1-yard) packages of black ruffle elastic, such as Dritz foldover elastic (amount depends on the measurement of the cut neckline and hem)

2 or 3 (⅝-in. by 1-yard) packages of white ruffle elastic, such as Dritz foldover elastic (amount depends on the measurement of the cut neckline)

1 (1½-in. by 9-foot) spool of 100 percent polyester satin-type ribbon, such as Offray brand

Matching thread for T-shirts and trims

TOOLS

Pins

Cutting mat

Right-angle ruler and straightedge ruler or yardstick

Rotary cutter

Sewing machine

Scissors

---

1. Mark the back of both T-shirts by placing a pin on one sleeve of each. You will not be cutting the sleeves, but you will need to remember which side of the shirt is the back.

2. Position the black T-shirt face up on the cutting mat. Place the white T-shirt on top, face down, so the front sides are together. The back side of one shirt should be touching the mat and the back side of the other shirt should be facing you. Flatten out any wrinkles, perfectly matching the T-shirts so that when you cut the necklines, they are symmetrical. Align the bottom edges of the T-shirts together, and make sure that all of the HPSs are at the same line on the mat; use a few pins to keep the T-shirts in place. If you have some paperweights, those are fairly effective as well.

3. Find the HPS and place a pin roughly 2 in. away from it on the shoulder seam, pinning through both shirts at the same time. Find the opposite side of the shirt from where you just pinned and measure about 6 in. down from the underarm. Place another pin to mark the position, again pinning through both shirts. Position a straightedge ruler or yardstick between the two pins **(Figure A)**. Cut a diagonal line through all layers of the two tees using a rotary cutter **(Figure B)**.

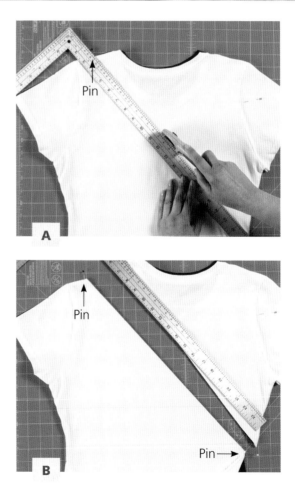

4. Remove the white T-shirt and set it aside. Next, cut the manufacturer's hem off the black T-shirt, just above the sewing line, to make a clean, straight raw edge. Do this by using a straightedge ruler and rotary cutter. This step serves two purposes: Cutting off the manufacturer's hem makes the black T-shirt slightly shorter than the white once assembled, and it makes the hem of the black portion nice and flat for placing the ruler in the next step.

5. Place the short edge of the right-angle ruler on the raw edge of the cut neckline so that the long edge of the ruler lands at the exact point where the hemline meets the side seam on the left side. This positioning is critical for creating a sharp point on both the front and the back of the black T-shirt where you will attach ribbons. Make sure you are creating a right angle, as shown; you may need to slide the ruler up and down the neckline until you find the correct position. Cut with a rotary cutter through both layers of the black T-shirt **(Figure C)**. Reposition the white T-shirt inside of the black T-shirt, as shown **(Figure D)**.

6. With matching threads and elastics, sew the ruffled elastic (black elastic on black shirt and white elastic on white shirt) along all raw edges of the two T-shirts using a sewing machine set on a three-step zigzag stitch. When applying the elastic on the sharp points on the front and back of the black portion of the T-shirt, be sure to turn the cut ends of the elastics under so the raw edges of the elastics end up on the inside of the T-shirt. You want your points to look neat because the ribbon will be placed there, drawing the eye. Trim any threads.

7. To keep the top in place when you are wearing it, you will need to connect the two tees together at the side seam. To do this, pin them together at the side seam about 9 in. up from the hem. Use a sewing machine to sew a stretch stitch through the two T-shirts at the side seam, from the pin to the hem.

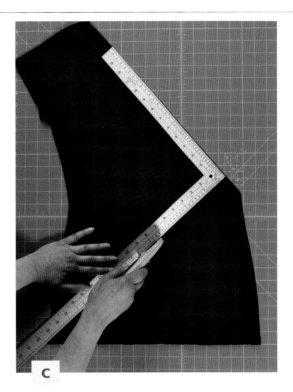

C

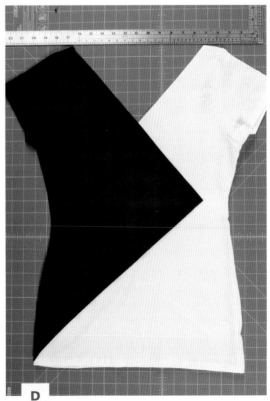

D

8. Place the connected T-shirt halves on the large cutting mat with the back of the shirts facing up; the pins you placed on the sleeves earlier indicate the back. Flatten out any wrinkles so the connected T-shirt halves are perfectly aligned in the front and back. Align the bottom edges of the white T-shirt with one of the gridlines on the mat and make sure both of the HPSs are at the same line on the mat. Place a pin where the white T-shirt half meets the black T-shirt half at the V and make a hand-stitched tack at that pin. The shirts are now connected at the sides and the back V neck.

9. Place the shirt on the cutting mat, back side up, and smooth and flatten it as before. Position a length of ribbon on the back of the garment in the V, as shown, approx. 2 in. down from the HPS; cut the ribbon, leaving it about 1 in. longer than the width of the V on either side so the raw edges don't show. Pin the ribbon to the sides of the V neck **(Figure E)**. **Note:** I used a 12-in. length of ribbon on a large T-shirt; adjust the measurement to fit your T-shirt, if necessary. Remember to make sure the raw edges of the ribbon don't show and that there is enough ribbon inside the garment to account for the angle of the V.

10. Next place a second length of ribbon approx. 2 in. below the first ribbon, long enough to be inserted and caught when sewn onto the V on either side. Pin the ribbon to the sides of the V neck **(Figure E)**. **Note:** I used a 6-in. length of ribbon on a large T-shirt; adjust the measurement to your T-shirt, if necessary. Remember to make sure the raw edges of the ribbon don't show and that there is enough ribbon inside the garment to account for the angle of the V. Sew the ribbons in place along the ruffled elastic for about 1 in. to secure. I used a stretch stitch on the sewing machine.

11. Cut two lengths of ribbon approx. 24 in. long. Place the raw edges of the ribbon under the pointed edges of the black T-shirt and pin in place. I used white thread and a white bobbin on the white side of the T-shirt and black thread and a white bobbin on the black side of the T-shirt. I used a three-step zigzag stitch and went right over the elastic, capturing the ribbon. Trim the ribbon neatly. Put the T-shirt on, tying the ribbons at your waist as shown.

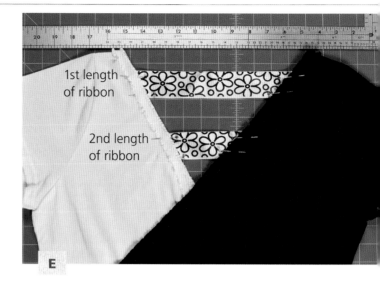

1st length of ribbon

2nd length of ribbon

E

variation

For a really interesting twist on this project, why not try two concert T-shirts from your favorite band? We all have them in our closets, and this could be a cool way to get them off of the shelf and out in public.

DAISY CHAIN

The look that inspired this tee is a runway favorite. It's so easy and affordable that you can experiment with different types of lace ribbons to create a look entirely your own. Why stop at just one? You can make a different look for every occasion by simply changing up the color or style of your trim.

EXPERIENCE LEVEL

Beginner

MATERIALS

White 100 percent cotton T-shirt, such as Jerzees ladies junior fit style (shown in size large)

Approx. 2 yards of flowered netting trim, such as 3-in.-wide 100 percent polyester Simplicity Apparel and Craft daisy ribbon trim

1 (⅝-in. by 20-foot) package of washable double-sided permanent adhesive fabric tape, such as PeelnStick Fabric Fuse

Matching thread for T-shirt and trim

TOOLS

Pins

Cutting mat

Straightedge ruler or yardstick

Rotary cutter

Sewing machine

Hand-sewing needle

Scissors

1. Mark the center front of the garment with a pin, 6 in. to 7 in. down, depending on how deep you would like your neckline. The depth of the plunge is your preference. I suggest putting the T-shirt on and seeing just how low you would like to go for your own personal style.

2. Remove the garment and place it on the cutting mat. Flatten out any wrinkles, perfectly matching the T-shirt front and back so that when you cut the neckline, it is symmetrical. Align the bottom edges of the T-shirt together and with one of the gridlines on the mat; use a few pins to keep the T-shirt in place. If you have some paperweights, those are fairly effective as well. Just make sure that both of the HPSs are at the same line on the mat.

variation

If you want to go for an even more dramatic look, double the rows of daisy ribbon trim on the neckline or fill the gap in the back V neck with additional rows of trim.

3. Mark the shoulder approx. 1½ in. from the neckline with a pin. Position a straightedge ruler between the center front pin and the shoulder pin and cut a deep V through both the front and the back of the T-shirt **(Figure A)**. Flip over the first cut and align to the opposite side. Place the ruler on the raw edge and mimic the cut in the same manner **(Figure B)**. You will now have a deep V in the front and back of the shirt **(Figure C)**.

4. Using a sewing machine, matching thread, and an overcast setting, sew the edges of the neckline to stabilize them and to prevent them from unraveling or curling. Measure your neckline (front and back) and cut a length of daisy ribbon trim to match this length (plus 1 in. or 2 in. for overlap). Following the manufacturer's instructions, apply the double-sided fabric adhesive tape to the trim along the neckline (this is easier and more accurate than basting). Sew the daisy ribbon trim by hand along the neckline in inconspicuous areas. You should start on one side of the front neckline point, move around the back of the shirt, and finish sewing on the opposite side of the front neckline point. Slightly overlap the final length of trim over your starting point to hide any gap.

tip

Sewing by hand ensures that you don't crush the flowers with your sewing machine. Be sure not to sew through the adhesive tape, however, which will leave a residue on your needle and thread.

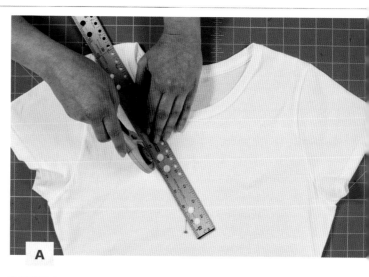

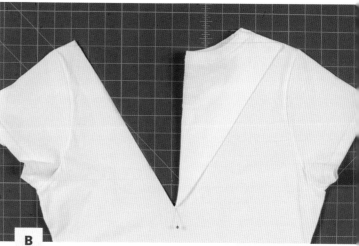

5. Find the spot in the back neckline that you would like to place a strip of daisy ribbon trim and mark this spot with a pin on each side of the neckline. (I placed mine 3 in. down from the HPS, but you can place yours wherever is most comfortable) **(Figure D)**. Measure across the neckline from this point so you know how much trim you need. **Note:** I used approx. 9 in. of trim on a large T-shirt; adjust the measurement to your T-shirt, if necessary. Position the length of daisy ribbon trim across the back V neck at your marked location. Sew the trim at each edge by hand with some small tacks.

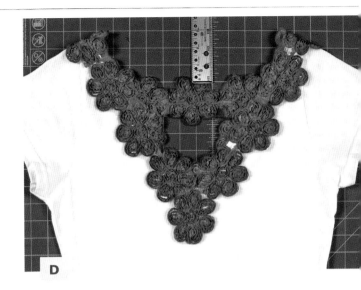

D

LOVE LETTERS

Do you love fashion? Then shout it out! This T-shirt offers two great ways for you to express yourself. The front features alphabet charms that can spell out any message you want, and the back features a dramatic heart-shaped cutout.

EXPERIENCE LEVEL

Advanced

MATERIALS

Black 100 percent cotton T-shirt, such as Jerzees ladies junior fit style (shown in size large)

1 or 2 (⅝-in. by 1-yard) packages of contrasting color ruffle elastic, such as Dritz foldover elastic, shown in neon pink no. 9388 (amount depends on the size of your heart cutout and arrow)

Glamour charms in various letters (to spell out your personal message), such as Blue Moon Beads® Impressions charms

Matching thread for the T-shirt and trim

TOOLS

Small cutting mat

Template paper

Scissors

Rotary cutter

French curve or flexible ruler

Sewing machine

Pins

Hand-sewing needle

1. Place a small cutting mat inside the T-shirt so that you only cut through one layer of the fabric. The back of the tee should be facing up. Smooth out any wrinkles in the T-shirt. Draw a heart shape on paper and cut it out to create a template.

2. Position the paper heart in the center of the back, taking care to make sure it is not overlapping the neckline. Carefully cut around one side of the heart template using the rotary cutter and French curve, moving the French curve as needed to cut accurate curves **(Figures A and B)**.

tip

Be sure you hold the template perfectly still while cutting around it. You can pin it in place if desired.

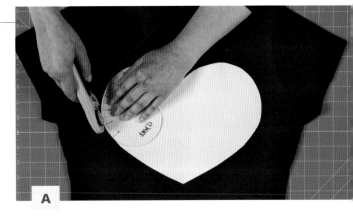

A

B

3. After you've finished the first half of the heart, remove the template and flip over the first cut portion. Repeat the cutting technique on the other half of the heart **(Figure C)**. You will end up with a heart-shaped hole in the back of your T-shirt.

4. Using a sewing machine and matching thread, sew along the raw edge of the heart with a stretch stitch or overcast stitch, taking care not to tug or pull on the edge. The sewing will give some stability to the cut edge and prevent it from unraveling, while also helping to keep the fabric in place when you attach the ruffle elastic. Measure around the heart-shaped hole and cut a length of ruffle elastic that matches this measurement plus 1 in. extra. Pin the elastic to the edge of the heart. Starting on one side of the heart's point, sew the elastic in place with a sewing machine using a three-step zigzag stitch. Finish on the other side of the heart's point, taking care to overlap the elastic ends neatly.

5. Cut a length of elastic for the body of the arrow that is long enough to reach across the heart. **Note:** I used approx. 15 in. of elastic for my heart; adjust the measurement to your cutout, if necessary. Using a three-step zigzag stitch and matching thread, stitch the body of the arrow in place. Make sure you only attach the arrow to the back of the T-shirt. Cut 4 additional lengths of elastic, each measuring 2½ in., and use these to create the point and the tail of the arrow **(Figures D and E)**.

tip

The body of the arrow should lie flat across the heart but not be stretched. When you wear the shirt, the body of the arrow will pull into place.

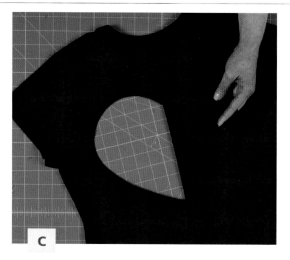

C

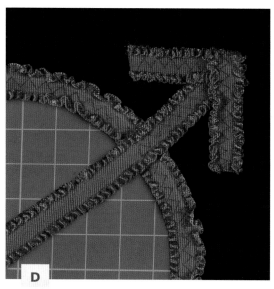

D

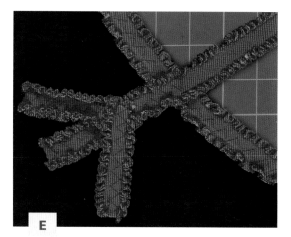

E

6. Turn the shirt to the front and spell out a fabulous fashion slogan using the alphabet charms. Sew the charms to the shirt by hand with matching thread. You can always try using vintage charms as well, if you have those at hand. Creativity and surprises are what fashion is about. Imagine wearing the T-shirt under a cute jacket for a night on the town, the words peeking out playfully: What do they say? Then take off the jacket when you hit the dance floor to reveal the open heart back. *Wow!*

variation

If an open back is not your thing, sew some lace to the inside of the heart, or attach a ribbon heart to the T-shirt front without the arrow and sew your charms into the center. Any message will work—why not try "I Heart Fashion" or "Fashion Is Love"? Or you can express your love of a favorite band, movie, or designer. Try anything you like.

UPTOWN CHIC TEE

There is beauty in simplicity, and this tee certainly proves it. Just cut two lengths of ruffled fabric, cross them on the front and back of your shirt, and hand-stitch them in place to create an ethereal quality that is sure to be noticed.

EXPERIENCE LEVEL

Intermediate

MATERIALS

White V-neck T-shirt, such as Champion loose-fit Active Performance (shown in size medium)

1 or 2 packages (⅞-in. by 1-yard) of sheer ruffle elastic, such as Dritz sheer ruffle elastic no. E-3, shown in snow (the amount depends on the circumference of the T-shirt hem)

½ yard of 50-in.-wide 100 percent polyester ruffle knit fabric, shown in white

Matching thread for T-shirt and trims

TOOLS

Rotary cutter

Right-angle ruler and straightedge ruler or yardstick

Scissors

Cutting mat

Pins

Sewing machine

Hand-sewing needle

1. Using a rotary cutter and a straightedge ruler, cut the ruffle knit fabric to create 2 strips, each measuring 8 in. by 50 in. Cut through the plain flat areas of the knit and be careful not to damage any ruffles while cutting. Place each strip of ruffle knit fabric on the cutting mat and mark the center of the top edge of each with a pin, indicating the halfway point of the short edge. This will mark where to place the ruffle knit fabric on the HPS. Position the T-shirt on the cutting mat facing up.

2. Flatten out any wrinkles, perfectly matching the T-shirt front and back so that when you cut the hem, it is symmetrical. Align the bottom edges of the T-shirt together and with one of the gridlines on the mat; use a few pins to keep the T-shirt in place. If you have some paperweights, those are fairly effective as well. Just make sure that both of the HPSs are at the same line on the mat.

tip

I've found that there are two different types of ruffled fabric available at most craft stores. One is manufactured with the ruffles parallel to the selvage and the other is manufactured with the ruffles across the grain, perpendicular to the selvage. For this project, I used the type with the ruffles perpendicular to the selvage so that the ruffles would flutter as the body moves.

3. Using a straightedge ruler, cut off the manufacturer's hem. Using a sewing machine and a three-step zigzag stitch, sew the ruffled elastic to the hemline, turning the raw ends under at the end of the run for a clean and neat finish **(Figure A)**. Trim any threads.

4. Position the strips of the ruffle knit fabric in a crisscross shape over the front of the T-shirt, aligning the pins that are on the center of the top edge of the ruffles with the HPSs **(Figure B)**. Pin the fabric sections to the front V neck at the crisscross. Pin the ruffle knit fabric where each section meets at the sides to the side seams. Pin along the shoulder seams. While pinning in these spots, make sure you catch only one layer of the T-shirt fabric.

A

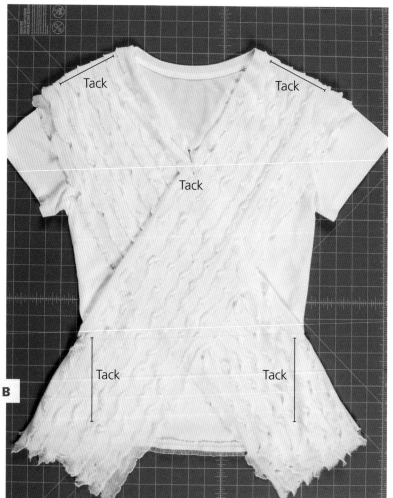

Tack Tack Tack Tack Tack

B

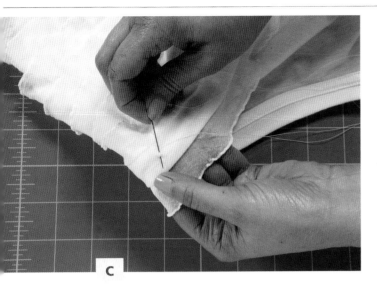

C

5. Flip the T-shirt over to the back side. Flatten out any wrinkles, perfectly matching the T-shirt front and back, and crisscross the two lengths of ruffle knit fabric, pinning at the side seams, as before.

6. Hand-sew tacks under the ruffles near the neckline, across the shoulders, and at the side seams where the ruffles meet **(Figures B** and **C)**. Allow the other areas to hang freely. This beautiful look is certainly uptown chic.

variation

For a variation, how about using a long-sleeve black T-shirt with black ruffle knit fabric? It would make for a great evening look paired with a sequined skirt.

LITTLE BLACK TEE

This little black tee will become one of your go-to looks. It can be dressed up or down depending on your needs, meaning you can wear it anywhere. Try it with strappy sandals and jeans for a casual look, or over leggings for a night on the town.

EXPERIENCE LEVEL

Advanced

MATERIALS

Black 100 percent cotton T-shirt, such as Jerzees ladies junior fit style (shown in size large)

Approx. 4 yards of 4-in.-wide ruffled organza with a satin ribbon edge, such as Simplicity brand (100 percent nylon), shown in black

Matching thread for T-shirt and trim

TOOLS

Large and small cutting mats

Pins

Rotary cutter

Right-angle ruler and straightedge ruler or yardstick

French curve or flexible ruler

Sewing machine

Scissors

Hand-sewing needle

tip

I used 4 yards of ruffled trim for this project, but you will need to buy enough to go around the garment as described in the instructions. I suggest you first alter the T-shirt and then measure the total sweep of edges to be trimmed, as shown in the figures. Be sure to add a little extra to account for the overlapped areas and seam allowances.

1. Position the T-shirt facing up on cutting mat. Flatten out any wrinkles, perfectly matching the T-shirt front and back so that when you cut the hem, it is symmetrical. Align the bottom edges of the T-shirt together and with one of the gridlines on the mat; use a few pins to keep the T-shirt in place. If you have some paperweights, those are fairly effective as well. Just make sure that both of the HPSs are at the same line on the mat.

2. Using a rotary cutter and a straightedge ruler, cut off the manufacturer's hemline. You want a crisp, straight raw edge to work with. Make sure to cut through both layers of the tee.

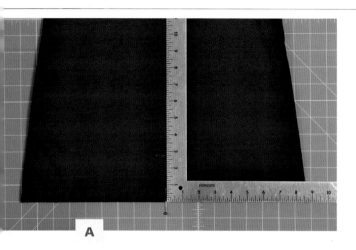

A

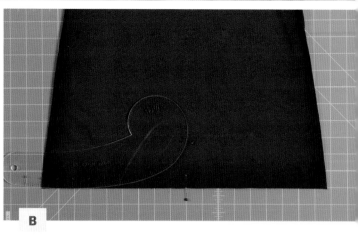

B

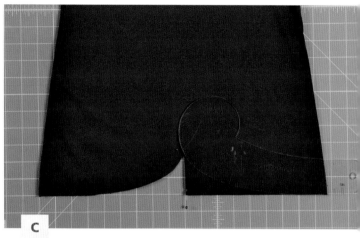

C

3. Next mark the center of the hem with a pin on the front of the T-shirt. Using a right-angle ruler, measure up 2¾ in. from the hem where you just placed the pin **(Figure A)**. Place another pin. If using a woven trim like the one shown, you will need to make sure the sweep of the French curve is deep enough to account for getting the shirt over your hips. For my T-shirt, 2¾ in. added a lot of extra room to the bottom hem. Position the French curve along the bottom hem on the far left side seam and rotate it until it touches the center higher pin, creating a pleasing sweep **(Figure B)**. Cut through both layers of the T-shirt using a rotary cutter.

4. Flip the cut piece to the other side and position it exactly symmetrical. Place the French curve or flexible ruler on top of the flipped cut piece to mimic the line in the same way. Use your rotary cutter to cut the mirror-image curve **(Figure C).** You will now have a tulip-shaped cut hemline **(Figure D)**.

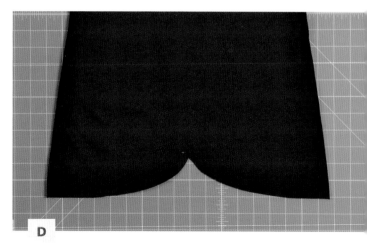

D

5. Pin the organza trim along the raw edge of the right side of the tulip hem (as it is facing you on the board). Be sure to pin all along the cut edge to the back side, ending the trim at the inside point on the back of the shirt, as shown. Be sure you have a little excess trim at the beginning and the end so you can catch it when you place the next length of trim. You want your ends to look neat. Trim any threads. You now have one side of the tulip pinned with the organza trim **(Figure E)**.

6. Using a sewing machine and a stretch stitch for a stretch trim or an overcast stitch for a woven trim, sew along the ribbon portion of the ruffle (this may vary depending on your trim).

7. Measure up from the bottom hem 9 in. along the right side seam and place another pin. Pin the organza trim starting at the marked pin that you have placed on the side seam and position it so that it wraps around the entire remaining cut hemline to the back, ending at the marked pin again. Pin the organza in place as you go, as shown **(Figure F)**.

8. Using a sewing machine and a stretch stitch for a stretch trim or an overcast stitch for a woven trim, sew along the ribbon portion of the ruffle (this may vary depending on your trim). Overlap the edges at the end of the run. You want your ends to look neat. Trim any threads.

9. Next place the T-shirt on the cutting mat as before and place a ruler in the center of the front neck, measuring down 8 in. from the HPS, as shown, or to a point that is comfortable for you. **Note:** If you have chosen a woven trim such as the one I used, the neckline will not stretch, so make sure that the neck opening is large enough for you to fit your head through without stretching the fabric. Place a pin on the 8-in. measurement, in the exact center of the front **(Figure G)**.

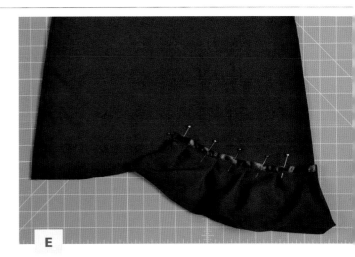

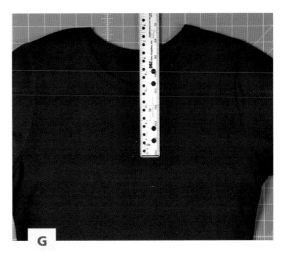

10. Using scissors, cut off the manufacturer's ribbed collar along the stitching line where it's attached to the body of the tee. Place a small cutting mat inside the front of the T-shirt and position the tee on the large cutting mat, smoothing out any wrinkles. Place a pin 2 in. away from the HPS on the shoulder seam. Place a ruler between the pin that is in the center front and the pin that is on the shoulder seam, creating an angle **(Figure H)**. Cut along the ruler with a rotary cutter. **Note:** You are cutting through only the front of the shirt, which is why the small cutting mat is inside the shirt. Take care that you have positioned the cutting board correctly. Repeat on the opposite side. You now have a deep V in the front of the shirt **(Figure I)**.

11. Flip the shirt over and assess the back neckline. You may have to recut the curve of the back neckline slightly to match up the cut made at the HPS. Use a French curve and a rotary cutter and be sure to reinsert the small cutting mat between the layers before you make the cuts. You can see the resulting neckline in **Figure J**.

H

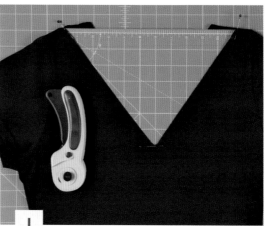

I

variation

If you want to modify and trim only the neckline or only the hem, the look will be a little more casual and would be great with leggings or jeans. Just make sure the curves you create allow the garment to go over your head and your hips. I suggest trying the garment on after you make your cuts and with the trim pinned on to see if the openings work for you, in case you need to adjust anything. Some trims won't stretch as much as the T-shirt, so it's better to know before you sew everything in place!

J

12. Remove the small cutting board and flip the tee so that the front side is facing up. Next attach the end of the ruffle to the point of the V neck, starting on the LSW of the garment. Pin around the back neckline and to the front, stopping at the RSW point of the V neck again. The lower part of the ruffle will hang freely until it is connected at the side seam. This is to account for the outward curve of different body types once the shirt is put on **(Figure J)**.

13. Using a sewing machine and a stretch stitch for a stretch trim or an overcast stitch for a woven trim, sew along the ribbon portion of the ruffle along the V neck. Overlap the edges at the end of the run. You want your ends to look neat. You will need to sew the ruffle to the V neck first, then try on the garment to see where you want to connect the loose part of the ruffle to the side seam. Mine is connected to the side seam starting at 5 in. below the LSW underarm and is stitched to the side seam using a stretch stitch. You could hand-stitch the trim in place, if you prefer. Trim any threads. You are ready to Rumba!

SILVER LININGS

Flowing vests over T-shirts are everywhere these days. This project combines the two pieces into a single garment that you can easily slip into on your way out of the house. Wear the vest open or, to change things up, throw one of the sections over your shoulder or loosely knot the vest in front.

EXPERIENCE LEVEL	MATERIALS	TOOLS
Beginner	Gray heather V-neck T-shirt Such as Champion loose-fit Active Performance (shown in size medium)	Scissors
		Rotary cutter
	1 yard of 57-in.-wide 98 percent polyester, 1 percent spandex, 1 percent other stretch ruffle knit fabric, shown in charcoal silver	Cutting mat
		Straightedge ruler or yardstick
	Matching thread for trim	Pins
		Sewing machine

1. Lay out the stretch ruffle fabric and cut it exactly in half vertically, perpendicular to the selvage edge (dividing the width in half). You should have two equal rectangles of fabric measuring 18 in. by 57 in. If 57 in. is too long for you, trim it to any length you like. Depending on your fabric choice, you may use scissors or a rotary cutter and a mat to cut the two rectangles.

2. Position the T-shirt facing up on the cutting mat. Flatten out any wrinkles, perfectly matching the T-shirt front and back. Align the bottom edges of the T-shirt together and with one of the gridlines on the mat; use a few pins to keep the T-shirt in place. If you have some paperweights, those are fairly effective as well. Just make sure that both of the HPSs are at the same line on the mat.

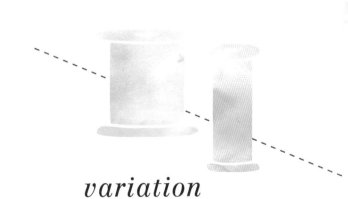

variation

You can create this look with just about any knit fabric or stretch lace. Just make sure to hem the three sides if the fabric is the kind that will unravel before you place the rectangles onto the shirt to sew.

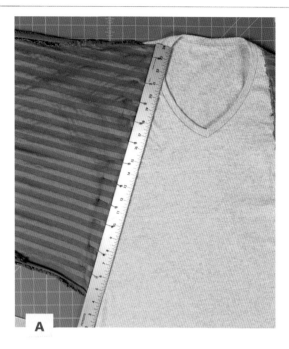

A

3. Place a straightedge ruler on top of one side of the T-shirt so the ruler begins at the HPS and travels down to the side seam at an angle. You will use the top edge of the ruler as a guide to position the short side of the ruffle knit fabric. Make sure the wrong side of ruffle knit fabric is face up because you are going to sew the inside of the ruffle so that when it flips over on body, you do not see the stitching. Pin along the short edge of one length of the ruffle knit fabric to connect it to the front layer of the T-shirt (**Figure A**). Take care to make sure the ruffles are pointing downward toward the hem.

4. Using a sewing machine and matching thread, sew the ruffle knit fabric in place (through the front layer of the T-shirt only) with an overcast stitch. Repeat on the other side of the shirt with the remaining ruffle fabric, to create a mirror image.

5. Trim all threads. The fabric I used will not unravel, so I chose not to finish the other edges, giving it a fashionable deconstructed look. If you are unsure about the fabric you are using, it is best to over-cast or hem the three sides of the rectangle before attaching the one short raw edge to the T-shirt.

FRAME YOUR FACE

This project is so simple that it's perfect for any last-minute invite you may get. All it takes is a few simple cuts and stitches, and you're ready to go. Depending on the trim you choose, you will stand out anywhere—whether a black-tie gala or a summer picnic.

MATERIALS

Black 100 percent cotton T-shirt, such as Jerzees ladies junior fit style (shown in size large)

Approx. 1 yard of decorative elastic trim, such as Simplicity Animal Print Elastic Flower trim (64 percent polyester, 36 percent elastic polyester), shown in brown leopard

Matching thread for T-shirt and trim

TOOLS

Cutting mat

Pins

French curve or flexible ruler

Rotary cutter

Sewing machine

Hand-sewing needle

Scissors

1. Position the T-shirt facing up on cutting mat. Flatten out any wrinkles, perfectly matching the T-shirt front and back so that when you cut the neckline, it is symmetrical. Align the bottom edges of the T-shirt together and with one of the gridlines on the mat; use a few pins to keep the T-shirt in place. If you have some paperweights, those are fairly effective as well. Just make sure that both of the HPSs are at the same line on the mat.

2. Measure and mark the center front of the neckline with a pin. Place your French curve or flexible ruler on one side of the pin, sweeping up to the shoulder in a gentle curve in a pleasing manner. Just be sure to leave about ½ in. of fabric on the shoulder seam—you want the sleeve to stay attached. Cut the curve using a rotary cutter, making sure to cut through both layers of the T-shirt **(Figure A)**. Flip over the cut piece to the other side of the neckline to create a mirror image of the sweep, and place the French curve or flexible ruler along the cut edge. Cut along the ruler to remove the remainder of the neckline **(Figure B)**.

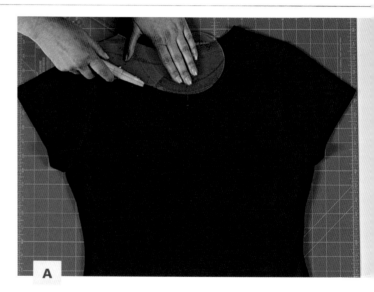

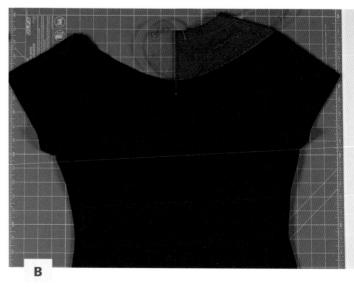

3. Using a sewing machine and matching thread, overcast the edge of the neckline to stabilize it. Measure around the neckline and cut a length of elastic trim, matching that length **Note:** I used a 36-in. length of ribbon on a large T-shirt; adjust the measurement to your T-shirt, if necessary. Pin the ribbon edging to the neckline **(Figure C)**. Sew the ribbon to the neckline along the edge using a hand stitch or tack in place, depending on your trim. A hand stitch will ensure you do not crush the delicate waves and flowers; however, if you picked a simpler trim, you can certainly use the sewing machine.

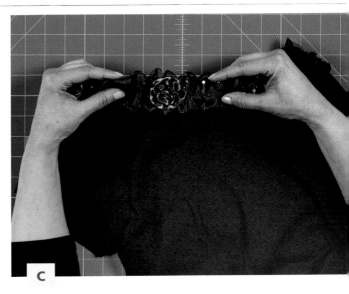

C

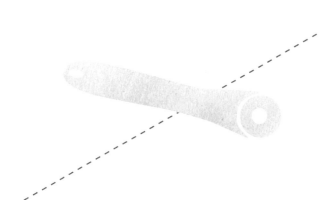

variation

You can find a world of trims at your local fabric store; just make sure the trim or ribbon you choose is slightly stretchy and/or that the neck opening that you cut fits over your head since T-shirts normally have a stretchy rib collar that expands.

SHOW ME SOME SKIN

It's easy to spice up a plain white tee into something that will make a statement. Just grab an accent fabric that expresses your personal style. (I chose a black and white cheetah print, but you can go with anything that strikes you.) The look is dramatic, but it takes just a couple of cuts and stitches, and you're all set.

EXPERIENCE LEVEL

Intermediate

MATERIALS

White 100 percent cotton V-neck T-shirt, such as Jerzees ladies junior fit style (shown in size large)

1 or 2 (⅝-in. by 1-yard) packages of matching shiny foldover elastic, such as Dritz shiny foldover elastic style no. 9389W, shown in white (amount depends on the measurement of the neckline)

1 yard of 58-in.-wide stretch print fabric, shown in an animal print (80 percent polyester, 20 percent spandex)

Matching thread for T-shirt and trims

TOOLS

Cutting mat

Right-angle ruler and straightedge ruler or yardstick

Pins

Rotary cutter

French curve or flexible ruler

Sewing machine

Scissors

1. Position the T-shirt facing up on the cutting mat. Flatten out any wrinkles, perfectly matching the T-shirt front and back. Align the bottom edges of the T-shirt together and with one of the gridlines on the mat; use a few pins to keep the T-shirt in place. If you have some paperweights, those are fairly effective as well. Just make sure that both of the HPSs are at the same line on the mat.

2. Place a right-angle ruler approx. 4 in. in from the right side seam, at the waist, and place the short edge of the ruler parallel to the hem. Measure up 14 in. from the hem and place a pin. Use a rotary cutter to cut a straight line along the long edge of the right-angle ruler, ending at the pin. Make sure you cut through both layers of the T-shirt **(Figure A)**.

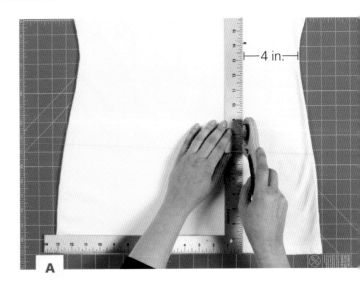

—4 in.—

A

B

C

3. Position a pin approx. 4 in. away from the cut, on the bottom hem. Use the ruler to connect the pins and create a right triangle; cut through both layers of the T-shirt along the ruler **(Figure B)**. You should now have an empty space in the T-shirt on both the front and the back of the shirt **(Figure C)**. Each will look like a right triangle (featuring a 90-degree angle).

4. Mark the center front of the neckline with a pin and then place another pin 2 in. away from the HPS on the shoulder seam. Place a French curve or flexible ruler in a pleasing and gentle slope, starting at the pin on the center front of the neckline and working up toward the shoulder pin. Using a rotary cutter, cut out a gentle curved neckline **(Figure D)**. Then flip over the cut piece to the uncut side so that you can mimic the curve on the opposite side, as shown **(Figure E)**. Align the French curve with the raw edge and cut the remainder of the neckline with a rotary cutter **(Figure F)**. This helps you cut the neckline accurately, ensuring a balanced, even opening.

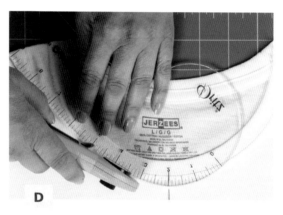

D

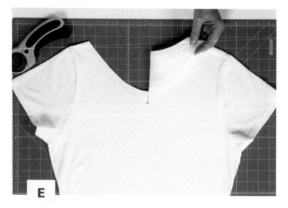

E

5. Pin the foldover elastic along the neckline with the raw edge of the neckline on the center of the elastic. Sew the elastic to the neckline using a sewing machine and a three-step zigzag stitch. Next fold the elastic over and topstitch the elastic using a sewing machine and a three-step zigzag stitch. Be sure to overlap the elastic's ends in the back of the neck for a neat finish.

6. Cut the animal print fabric into two rectangles, each measuring 36 in. by 29 in. Fold each piece in half lengthwise, wrong sides together, so it now measures 36 in. by 14½ in. Open up the right triangle on the front of the shirt. Pin the raw long edges of the print fabric to the cut edges of the shirt, letting the excess print fabric hang below the shirt **(Figure G)**. Be sure you pin the right side of the fabric to the right side of the T-shirt. Using a sewing machine and an overcast stitch, sew the print fabric to the T-shirt, removing pins as you sew **(Figure H)**. Repeat by attaching the remaining animal print rectangle to the right triangle cutout on the back side of the T-shirt. Overcast any remaining raw edges of the print fabric using the sewing machine. Trim the threads.

variation

If you want, you can make four inserts with four different animal prints for a super-fashionable tee. Animal skin not your thing? Try camouflage or a beautiful Japanese-style floral. It's up to you.

OVER THE TOP

Turn up the glamour factor of your wardrobe by adding a compelling scarf to a long-sleeved T-shirt. This easy-to-complete project can be made with a length of fabric from your local craft store or you can use a favorite scarf for an upcycled piece of fashion art.

EXPERIENCE LEVEL

Beginner

MATERIALS

White 90 percent cotton, 10 percent spandex long-sleeve T-shirt such as Champion loose-fit Active Performance (shown in size medium)

2 yards of 67-in.-wide lightweight striped stretch fabric, shown in a lacey stripe blue/ivory (85 percent polyester, 15 percent cotton)

Matching thread for T-shirt and trim

TOOLS

Scissors

Sewing machine

Pins

Right-angle ruler and straightedge ruler or yardstick

Rotary cutter

Large cutting mat

1. Measure and cut out a rectangle of fabric approx. 2 yards long by 1 yard wide. Using a sewing machine, matching thread, and a three-step zigzag or blind hemstitch, turn the edges in ½ in. twice and sew around all four sides to hem the rectangle (this will prevent the fabric from unraveling and will look neater).

2. Find the RSW of the T-shirt. Next, locate the RSW shoulder seam at the point where the sleeve is attached. Place the fabric rectangle face up onto the RSW of the shirt with the long sides positioned horizontally (parallel to the shirt's hem). Make sure the top edge of the rectangle falls over the shoulder toward the back, ½ in. past the RSW shoulder seam.

3. Pin the rectangle to the T-shirt along the shoulder seam to stabilize the rectangle while you are sewing.

tip

This project really requires you to try on the T-shirt as you alter it. If you are making this for a gift and not for yourself, try to use a friend that is the same size as the giftee as your tester. Or, you can make this into an event: Give your friend the chance to pick out the fabric and create the project together!

4. Using a sewing machine and a three-step zigzag stitch, sew along the pinned edge of the rectangle to attach the rectangle to the T-shirt at the RSW, removing pins as you sew. **Note:** The stitching line should be a ½ in. away from the shoulder seam but running parallel to the shoulder seam. Sew until you have reached about 1 in. away from the neck opening. This will allow the rectangular piece to have some stability without pulling the T-shirt forward when you wear it, because the connection point is slightly past the shoulder seam on the back of the garment **(Figure A)**.

5. Try on the T-shirt with the attached fabric. Position the short side of the rectangle against the RSW side seam of the T-shirt, allowing the rectangle to drape over the silhouette of your body.

6. Place one pin about 4 in. down from the underarm to connect the fabric rectangle to the T-shirt. This pin will indicate the beginning of where you will stitch the fabric to the side seam. Carefully remove the tee and continue placing pins downward from the first pin along the side seam to connect the short side of the rectangle to the T-shirt. Sew in place along the pinned edge using a three-step zigzag stitch on a sewing machine, removing the pins as you sew **(Figure B)**. **Note:** The upper portion of this side of the rectangle is not sewn and hangs freely over your silhouette. You don't want it to pull—you want it to drape, as shown in **Figure C**.

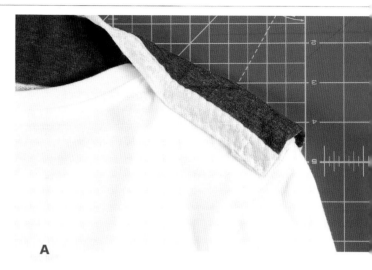

A

B

7. Place the T-shirt flat on a cutting mat with the front facing up. Place 1 pin 3 in. down from the HPS. Place a second pin 4 in. down and 3 in. to the right of the first pin. Create a slightly angled stitching line along the front of the T-shirt between these pins **(Figure C)**. Only do this on the RSW, so as to anchor the scarf piece and create a cowl effect. Try on the T-shirt.

8. Throw the length of the rectangle over the top of the LSW shoulder and position it to have a nice drape. Place a pin on the bottom edge of the rectangle where it meets the top of the sleeve and shoulder seam, as shown **(Figure D)**. Remove the tee and continue pinning along the shoulder seam for 2 in. to 3 in., depending on the size of the T-shirt. Sew in place along the pinned edge, using a three-step zigzag stitch on the sewing machine, removing pins as you sew.

9. Now you're ready to wear the T-shirt and *zhoosh* the scarf. You are over the top!

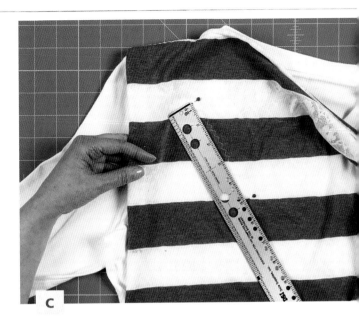

C

D

variation

For an evening look, why don't you try pairing an elegant sparkling fabric with a silver T-shirt? Or try a lightweight fabric with embellished accents; there are many beautiful choices of fabrics to use. Explore your creativity.

FRINGE BENEFITS

This project shows you some of the fringe benefits that come along with knowing how to sew: being able to create fun, fanciful garments without breaking the bank. An altered neckline and hem, cuts made to the T-shirt's sleeves, and a whole bunch of brightly colored fringe makes for a hippie-chic tee that you'll want to wear everywhere.

EXPERIENCE LEVEL	MATERIALS	TOOLS
Experienced	White 100 percent cotton T-shirt such as Jerzees ladies junior fit style (shown in size large)	Pins
		Cutting mat
	Approx. 3½ to 4 yards of 2-in.-wide fringe trim, such as Simplicity brand (95 percent rayon, 5 percent polyester)	French curve or flexible ruler
		Rotary cutter
	Matching thread for trim	Scissors
		Sewing machine
		Straightedge ruler or yardstick

1. Mark the back of the T-shirt with a pin somewhere in the middle of the back. You will not be cutting here, but you will need to remember which side is the back because the necklines will be the same depth on both the front and the back of the tee.

2. Position the T-shirt facing up on the cutting mat. Flatten out any wrinkles, perfectly matching the T-shirt front and back so that when you cut the neckline, it is symmetrical. Align the bottom edges of the T-shirt together and with one of the gridlines on the mat; use a few pins to keep the T-shirt in place. If you have some paperweights, those are fairly effective as well. Just make sure that both of the HPSs are at the same line on the mat.

tip

Fringe moves around a lot when you are working with it, and it can sometimes flip up and get caught in your stitches. To prevent this, when you are getting ready to sew the fringe to your shirt, place a small piece of cardboard or a ruler on top of the fringe. This will keep the individual bits of fringe from getting in the way of your sewing machine. Just be careful not to sew through the cardboard!

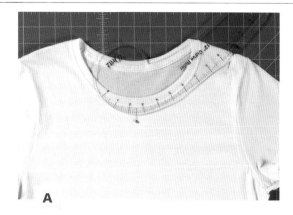

A

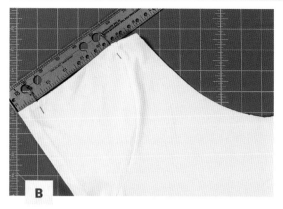

B

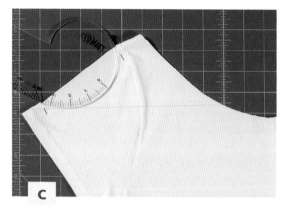

C

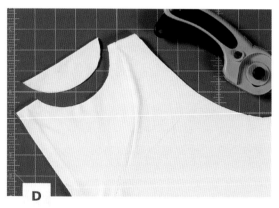

D

3. Find the top of the sleeve and place a pin roughly 1 in. out toward the neckline from the top of the sleeve and shoulder seam. Do the same on the other sleeve. Find the center of the neckline and place a pin. Using a French curve or flexible ruler, make a gentle sweep from the shoulder pin to the center front pin and cut with a rotary cutter through both layers of the shirt **(Figure A)**. Flip the cut piece to the opposite side of the center front and duplicate the same gentle sweep by placing the French curve or flexible ruler on top of the same cutting line. Now you have a gently sweeping neck opening.

4. Place a pin on the sleeve 1 in. below the top of the sleeve and shoulder seam. Place another pin 1 in. above the hem along the folded edge of the sleeve **(Figure B)**. Now place the French curve or flexible ruler between the two pins, creating a curve that connects them **(Figure C)**. Cut the curve out with a rotary cutter. You should now have a circular opening in the sleeve **(Figure D).** Repeat this process on the other sleeve. You can use the cut piece of fabric from the first sleeve to mimic the curve accurately on the other side; just position it in the same manner and use the French curve on top of it to create your cut.

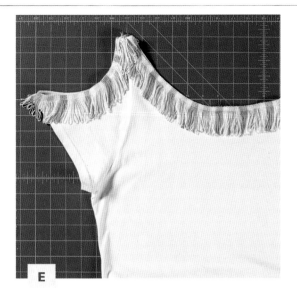

E

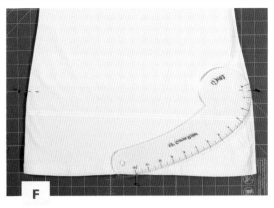

F

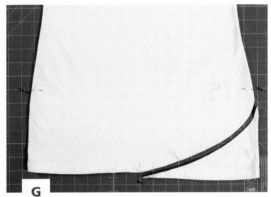

G

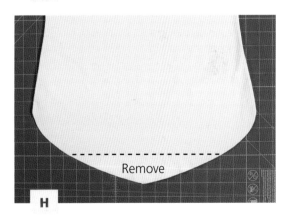

Remove

H

5. Measure along all of the raw edges of the upper half of the T-shirt (the areas you have cut—the front and back neckline and both sleeves). Cut three lengths of fringe according to these measurements, plus ½ in. for overlap. Using matching thread and a sewing machine, sew the fringe along the raw edges of the sleeve openings using a three-step zigzag stitch or a stretch stitch. Overlap the edges at the cut ends so that the raw edge of the fringe does not show. Next sew the fringe to the neckline, placing the overlap of the cut ends in the center of the back of the neck **(Figure E)**. Remember, you placed a pin on the back of the shirt to indicate the back. Trim any threads.

6. Measure up 6 in. from the hem on both side seams and place pins in those spots. Mark the center front of the hem with a pin. Using a French curve or flexible ruler, connect the center front pin and one of the side seam pins to make a gentle curve **(Figure F)**. Cut along the French curve with a rotary cutter **(Figure G)**. Flip the cut piece to the opposite side, positioning the French curve on top, and use the rotary cutter to make the cut. Cut off the remainder of the manufacturer's hemline using a straightedge ruler and rotary cutter **(Figure H)**.

7. Measure along all of the raw edges of your hem. Cut a length of fringe according to that measurement, plus ½ in. for overlap. Using matching thread and a sewing machine, sew the fringe along the raw edge of the hem using a three-step zigzag stitch or stretch stitch. Overlap the edges at the center back of the hem so that the raw edge of the fringe does not show. Trim any threads.

variation

There are so many varieties and lengths of fringe out there for you to try that you can change up this project to find a look that truly suits you. You can even mix up the fringe, try different color combinations, or get a leather-like fringe and apply it to a faux suede T-shirt. Any way you do it, variety is one of the fringe benefits of working with this trim.

A LITTLE BIT OF SWAGGER

Get yourself some fashion swagger by making this peek-a-boo tee and scarf top. A keyhole top lets you pass a scarf between the shirt's layers for a composed look that is sleek and eye-catching. Weave the scarf through one or both of the keyholes, depending on your style.

EXPERIENCE LEVEL	MATERIALS	TOOLS

EXPERIENCE LEVEL

Intermediate

MATERIALS

White 100 percent cotton V-neck T-shirt, such as Champion loose-fit Active Performance (shown in size medium) **Note:** For this project, I specifically recommend a loose-fit T-shirt.)

1 yard of 57-in.-wide chiffon fabric, such as Silky Prints crinkle chiffon, shown in zebra blue (100 percent polyester)

Matching thread for T-shirt and trim

TOOLS

Large and small cutting mats

Scissors

Sewing machine

Pins

Right-angle ruler

Rotary cutter

1. Lay the chiffon fabric on the cutting mat. Cut the fabric in half lengthwise, creating two long, thin rectangles. Using a straight stitch, sew the short end of one rectangle to the short end of the other rectangle to create a single long strip of fabric. You will now have a very long rectangle with a seam in the center. Place the right sides of the rectangle together and sew along the long side using a straight stitch. Turn the fabric right side out and fold the short edges in ¼ in. twice to create a small hem. Sew the hems using a straight stitch.

2. Position a small cutting mat inside the T-shirt and place the T-shirt face up on a large cutting mat. Flatten out any wrinkles, perfectly matching the T-shirt front and back so that when you cut the center front, it is straight. Align the bottom edges of the T-shirt together and with one of the gridlines on the mat; use a few pins to keep the T-shirt in place. If you have some paperweights, those are fairly effective as well. Just make sure that both of the HPSs are at the same line on the mat.

3. Find the center of the hem and mark it with a pin. Align the short end of a right-angle ruler with the hemline. Position the long end of the ruler between the lowest point of the V neck and the pin on the hem. Cut straight down the center front of the T-shirt along the long edge of the right-angle ruler using a rotary cutter.

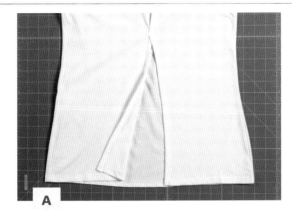

A

4. Fold the raw edges of the center front of the T-shirt in twice, making a ³⁄₈-in. turn each time. Pin in place until you have reached 14 in. up from the bottom hem. With matching thread and a sewing machine, use a stretch stitch to sew along the folded edge, up to the marked pin **(Figure A)**. If you prefer, hand-sew the front edges. Overlap the sewn center front edges by ³⁄₈ in. at the pinned spot and tack by machine to reconnect the center front. Overlap the T-shirt at the V neck and tack in place. Turn the T-shirt inside out and measure the distance between the V-neck tack and the center-front tack. Divide the measure in half and sew the center front raw edges together using a sewing machine and a stretch stitch or hand-sew for 1 in. This will create two keyholes in the center front of the shirt **(Figure B)**. Trim the threads.

5. Turn the T-shirt right side out and place the scarf through lower keyhole from the front of the garment to the inside so that the scarf's ends hang inside the tee **(Figure C)**.

Tack

Tack

B

C

variation

You can make the scarf as given in the ≠instructions or use different premade scarves from you own wardrobe to create a whole lot of swagger!

RESOURCES

JO-ANN FABRICS® STORES
www.joann.com

MICHAELS®
www.michaels.com

HOBBY LOBBY®
www.hobbylobby.com

A.C. MOORE
www.acmoore.com

WALMART®
www.walmart.com

ETSY™
www.etsy.com

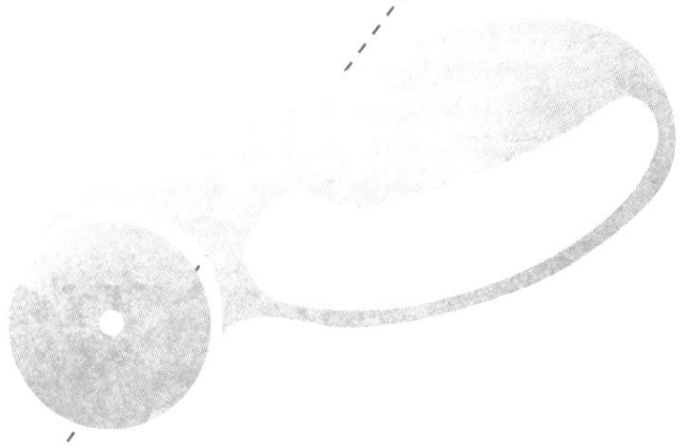

INSPIRATION

I find inspiration and fashion trends everywhere I look—whether it is on a trip to New York City, a day in a college town, or a walk down the street. I am always looking at how artists, designers, and even the general public express themselves, and I look at how they combine different colors and fabrics to create a statement. Don't be afraid to take a similar approach in your own designs. Use the techniques you've learned from the projects in this book to create your own unique tees.

If you notice something by your favorite designer that you just love, don't shy away from trying to replicate it at home. Just be sure that you put a little bit of yourself in there too. Remember, imitation is a sincere form of flattery!

METRIC EQUIVALENTS`

One inch equals approximately 2.54 centimeters. To convert inches to centimeters, multiply the figure in inches by 2.54 and round off to the nearest half centimeter, or use the chart below, whose figures are rounded off (1 centimeter equals 10 millimeters).

$\frac{1}{8}$ in.	=	3 mm	9 in. = 23 cm
$\frac{1}{4}$ in.	=	6 mm	10 in. = 25.5 cm
$\frac{3}{8}$ in.	=	1 cm	12 in. = 30.5 cm
$\frac{1}{2}$ in.	=	1.3 cm	14 in. = 35.5 cm
$\frac{5}{8}$ in.	=	1.5 cm	15 in. = 38 cm
$\frac{3}{4}$ in.	=	2 cm	16 in. = 40.5 cm
$\frac{7}{8}$ in.	=	2.2 cm	18 in. = 45.5 cm
1 in.	=	2.5 cm	20 in. = 51 cm
2 in.	=	5 cm	21 in. = 53.5 cm
3 in.	=	7.5 cm	22 in. = 56 cm
4 in.	=	10 cm	24 in. = 61 cm
5 in.	=	12.5 cm	25 in. = 63.5 cm
6 in.	=	15 cm	36 in. = 92 cm
7 in.	=	18 cm	45 in. = 114.5 cm
8 in.	=	20.5 cm	60 in. = 152 cm

Discover the world of *Threads*.

Read *Threads* Magazine:

Your subscription includes six issues of *Threads* plus FREE tablet editions. Every issue is packed with up-to-the-minute fashions, useful techniques, and expert garment-sewing advice – all designed to help improve your skills and express your creativity.

Subscribe today at:
ThreadsMagazine.com/4Sub

Shop our *Threads* Online Store:

It's your destination for premium resources from the editors of America's best-loved sewing magazine, designers, and sewing instructors: how-to and design books, videos, and more.

Visit today at:
ThreadsMagazine.com/4More

Become a Threads Insider:

Join now and enjoy exclusive online benefits, including: instant videos, favorite articles, digital issues, pattern database, and more.

Discover more information online:
ThreadsMagazine.com/4Join

Get our FREE *Threads* e-Newsletter:

Keep up with what's current – the latest styles, patterns, and fabrics, plus free tips and advice from our *Threads* editors.

Sign up, it's free:
ThreadsMagazine.com/4Newsletter

The Taunton Press